THE
MAGNIFICENT
BOOK OF
BUTTERFLIES
AND MOTHS

THE MAGNIFICENT BOOK OF BUTTERFLIES AND MOTHS

ILLUSTRATED BY
Simon Treadwell

WRITTEN BY
Barbara Taylor

weldon**owen**

Written by Barbara Taylor
Illustrated by Simon Treadwell

weldon**owen**

Copyright © Weldon Owen Children's Books, 2024

Published by Weldon Owen Children's Books
An imprint of Weldon Owen International, L.P.
A subsidiary of Insight International, L.P.
PO Box 3088
San Rafael, CA 94912
www.insighteditions.com

CEO: Raoul Goff

Publisher: Sue Grabham
Art Director: Stuart Smith

Senior Editor: Pauline Savage
Designer: Jade Wheaton
Senior Production Manager: Greg Steffen

ISBN: 979-8-88674-033-2

Manufactured, printed, and assembled in China.
First printing, October 2023 TOP1023
27 26 25 24 23 5 4 3 2 1

Introduction

From rainforests, deserts, and wetlands to mountains, grasslands, and gardens, butterflies and moths live in almost every corner of the world. Scientists estimate that there are about 160,000 species of moths and about 17,500 species of butterflies alive today.

These incredible insects are similar, but there are several ways to tell them apart. Butterflies tend to be more colorful than moths. They fly during the day and have antennae, or feelers, that are thicker at the ends. Moths are usually duller, with furry bodies. They fly at night and have threadlike or feathery antennae. But there are always exceptions!

Butterflies and moths go through four stages in their life cycle. They begin as a tiny egg, from which a caterpillar hatches. This creature spends its life eating and sheds its skin several times as it grows. Then it becomes a pupa. This is when the caterpillar wraps itself with a covering and transforms into its final stage—an adult butterfly or moth.

The Magnificent Book of Butterflies and Moths introduces you to some of the world's most spectacular species. Meet a butterfly that is bigger than a human hand, a moth that drinks blood, and a caterpillar that looks like a lobster. Discover a pupa that squeaks, a butterfly that hisses, and a moth that has army camouflage.

Explore the magnificent world of butterflies and moths and become inspired to protect these fragile and beautiful insects.

Fact file

Lives: Eastern USA

Habitat: Deciduous woodlands

Wingspan: 3¾–6 in (9.5–15 cm)

Caterpillar length: 5–6 in (12.5–15 cm)

Moth lifespan: 1–2 weeks

Diet: Leaves of walnut, hickory, sweet gum, persimmon, sumac (caterpillar); no food (moth)

Contents

Apollo butterfly

Parnassius apollo

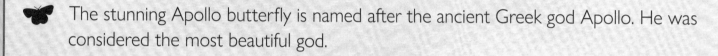

- The stunning Apollo butterfly is named after the ancient Greek god Apollo. He was considered the most beautiful god.

- The red or orange eyespots on the Apollo butterfly's wings scare predators such as birds. These false eyes also draw attention away from the butterfly's real eyes, which are essential for its survival.

- Female Apollo butterflies are bigger than the males. They produce special scents to attract males for mating.

- Apollo butterflies live in very cold climates. Their caterpillars form after three to four weeks in the egg, but they spend about another eight months inside in order to protect themselves from the long, harsh winters.

- Male Apollo butterflies patrol their own territory. They chase off any other males that invade it.

Fact file

Lives: Europe, Central Asia

Habitat: Mountain grasslands and rocky slopes, forests

Wingspan: female: 2½–3¾ in (6.5–9.5 cm); male: 2½–3½ in (6.2–8.6 cm)

Caterpillar length: 1½–2 in (4–5 cm)

Lifespan: About 1 year (caterpillar); a few weeks (butterfly)

Diet: Leaves of stonecrop, houseleek (caterpillar); flower nectar (butterfly)

The Apollo butterfly is rare in many parts of Europe, and in some places it has become extinct. In several countries, these butterflies are now protected by law.

Oleander hawk-moth

Daphnis nerii

▲ This moth's colors and patterns are similar to the camouflage uniforms worn by soldiers. These give the oleander hawk-moth its other name, the army green moth.

▲ The oleander hawk-moth has powerful streamlined wings that are shaped like the wings of a jet aircraft. These make the moth a fast flier, capable of reaching speeds of up to 12 mph (20 kmph).

▲ After sunset, this large hawk-moth hovers like a hummingbird in front of sweet-smelling flowers to feed on their nectar.

▲ The oleander hawk-moth's caterpillars feed mainly on the poisonous leaves of oleander plants. They eat the poisons without being harmed.

▲ The false eyes on both the adult moths and the caterpillars help to scare off predators.

▲ The caterpillars have a pointed horn at the end of their body, which helps prevent birds, bats, and lizards from attacking them.

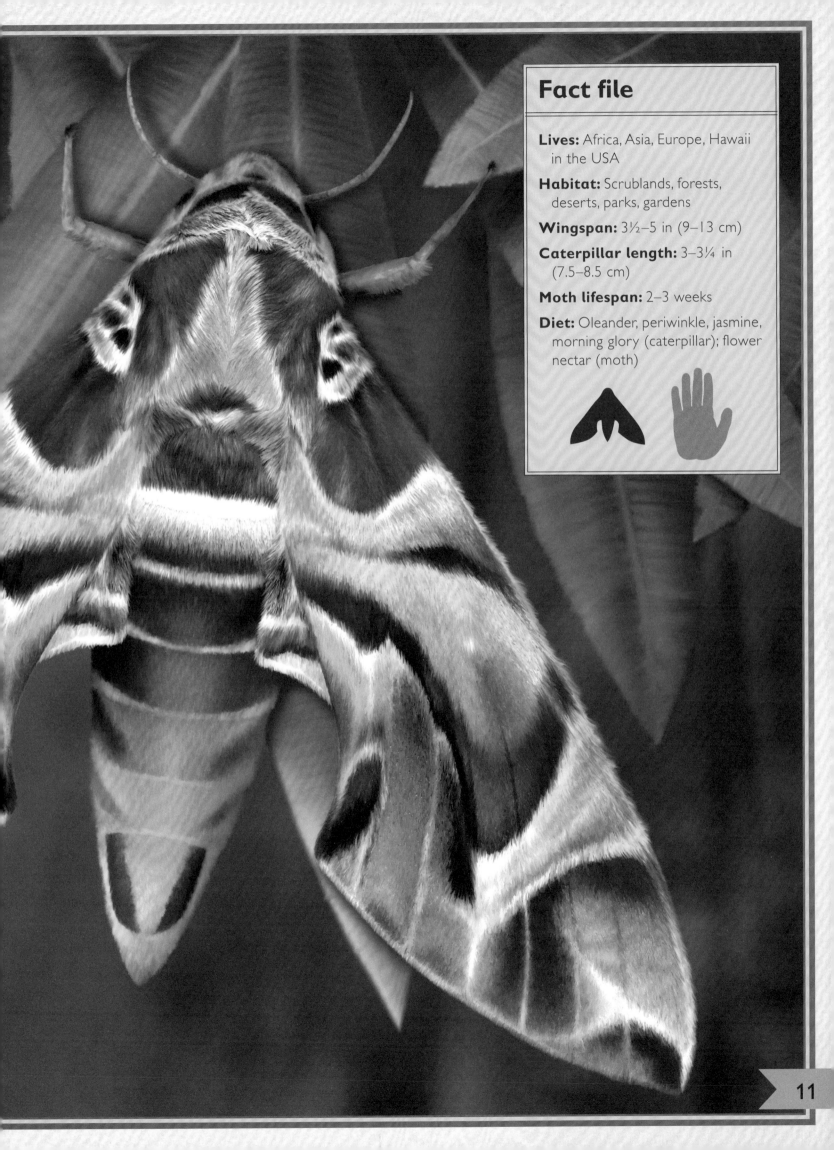

Fact file

Lives: Africa, Asia, Europe, Hawaii in the USA

Habitat: Scrublands, forests, deserts, parks, gardens

Wingspan: 3½–5 in (9–13 cm)

Caterpillar length: 3–3¼ in (7.5–8.5 cm)

Moth lifespan: 2–3 weeks

Diet: Oleander, periwinkle, jasmine, morning glory (caterpillar); flower nectar (moth)

Glasswing butterfly

Greta oto

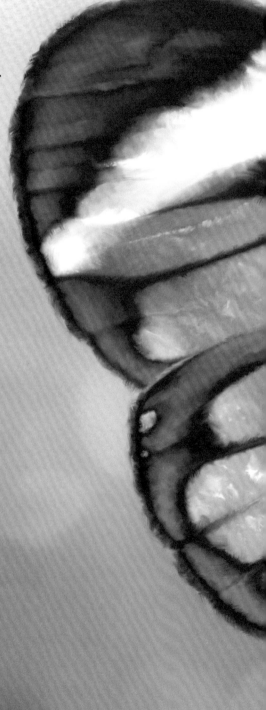

🦋 Many butterflies have colorful wings, but the wings of the glasswing are almost entirely see-through, just like panes of glass.

🦋 Transparent wings make these butterflies hard for predators to spot, especially when they fly in the dappled light and shade of the rainforest.

🦋 Glasswing butterflies migrate as the weather changes, or when they need to find fresh food for their caterpillars. The butterflies may travel up to 12 miles (19 km) in one day.

🦋 Glasswings look fragile but they are strong butterflies, able to carry nearly 40 times their own weight.

Fact file

Lives: Central and South America, Texas and Florida in the USA

Habitat: Rainforests

Wingspan: 2–2½ in (5.6–6.1 cm)

Caterpillar length: 1¼ in (3 cm)

Butterfly lifespan: 6–12 weeks

Diet: Nightshade leaves (caterpillar); flower nectar, bird droppings (butterfly)

Male glasswing butterflies sometimes flutter around together, spreading a special scent that attracts females for them to mate with. This behavior is called lekking.

To help it stay firmly attached to the underside of a leaf, the silver-colored glasswing chrysalis uses hooks to cling onto a sticky silk pad spun by the caterpillar.

Large blue butterfly

Phengaris arion

 The rare large blue butterfly is only as big as an adult's thumb. Even though it is small, it is the largest butterfly in the "blue" family—hence its name.

 When the large blue butterfly closes its wings, the camouflage colors on the undersides help it to hide in grasslands. The top sides of its wings are bright blue, with black spots on the front wings.

 Large blue caterpillars look and smell like red ant grubs. This fools adult ants into carrying the caterpillars to their underground nest for safety. Unfortunately for the ants, the caterpillars then feed on the actual ant grubs.

 The large blue caterpillar spends most of its life inside a red ant nest, where it is warm, is protected from predators, and has plenty of food to eat. After many months, it turns into a pupa and rests in the nest until it crawls out as a butterfly.

 All species of *Phengaris* butterflies are endangered due to climate change and habitat loss.

Fact file

Lives: Europe, Asia

Habitat: Grasslands, pastures

Wingspan: 1½–2 in (3.8–5.2 cm)

Caterpillar length: ½ in (1.3 cm)

Lifespan: 10–22 months (caterpillar); 7 days (butterfly)

Diet: Wild thyme, wild marjoram, ant grubs (caterpillar); flower nectar (butterfly)

Hercules moth

Coscinocera hercules

The Hercules moth is the largest moth in Australia and one of the largest in the world. Its wings have the greatest surface area of any insect.

This enormous moth is named after the ancient Roman hero Hercules. The mythical character is known for his superhuman strength.

The male Hercules moth's large, feathery antennae help him to detect the scent given off by females over a mile (2 km) away.

From the side, the Hercules moth's front wing tips look like snakes' heads. This scary disguise helps to stop predators such as birds from attacking these moths.

There are four transparent patches on the Hercules moth's giant wings. The surface it is resting on shows through, helping the moth to hide in its surroundings.

Hercules moth caterpillars have two false eyes on the back of their bodies. These markings draw attention away from their real eyes, which are at the front end.

Fact file

Lives: Northern Australia, New Guinea

Habitat: Rainforests

Wingspan: 10½–12 in (27–30 cm)

Caterpillar length: 4–4¾ in (10–12 cm)

Moth lifespan: 10–14 days

Diet: Bleeding heart tree, red bean tree, cheese tree, black cherry tree (caterpillar); no food (moth)

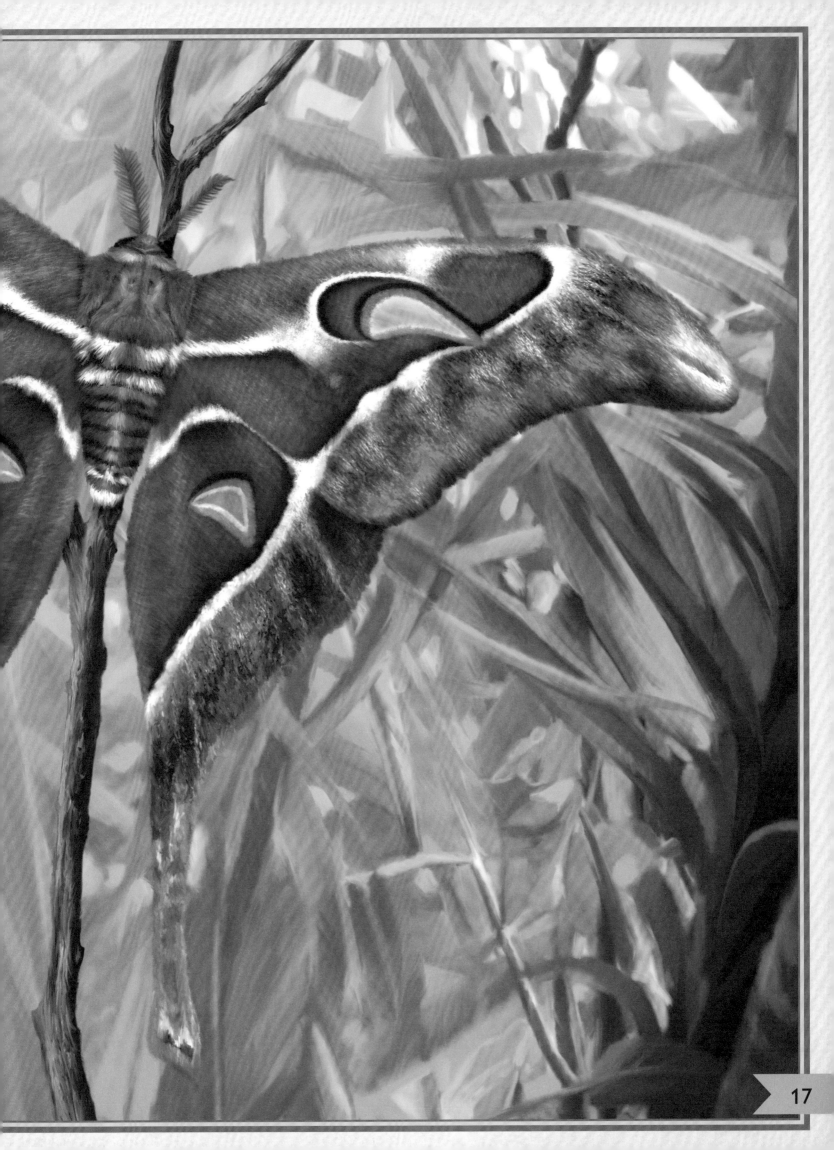

Paper kite butterfly

Idea leuconoe

- This large butterfly is called the paper kite or the rice paper butterfly. This is because of the way it slowly flutters and glides like a kite or a piece of thin paper drifting in the wind.

- The striking black-and-white colors of the paper kite butterfly and its caterpillar are a defense. They tell predators that they are poisonous.

- Paper kite caterpillars spit out a yellow foam as they are eating. This foam forms a protective ring around them, helping to keep predator ants away.

- The paper kite pupa develops inside a shiny golden chrysalis with 10 black spines underneath. The spines help to protect the chrysalis until the butterfly hatches.

Fact file

Lives: East and Southeast Asia

Habitat: Rainforests, mangrove swamps

Wingspan: 3¾–4½ in (9.5–11.4 cm)

Caterpillar length: 1.3 cm (½ in)

Butterfly lifespan: 1–3 weeks

Diet: Leaves of forest vines (caterpillar); flower nectar (butterfly)

When paper kite butterflies rest, they usually hold their wings open. This is unusual for butterflies, which tend to rest with their wings pressed together.

The paper kite butterfly is so big it will only just fit on an adult's hand. It is the largest butterfly found in Japan.

Green hairstreak butterfly

Callophrys rubi

- Green hairstreak butterflies are bright emerald green on the undersides of their wings. But the tops of their wings are a dull brown color, so they look brown when they fly.

- Hairstreak butterflies get their name from the very thin, hairlike streak across the undersides of their wings. In the green hairstreak, this line looks like a row of small white dots.

- Male green hairstreak butterflies have a pale patch of scent scales on the top of their front wings. The scents help the males to attract females for mating.

- Female green hairstreaks lay their eggs individually on the flower buds or shoots of the caterpillars' foodplants.

Fact file

Lives: Europe, North Africa, Asia

Habitat: Grasslands, woodlands, heathlands, moorlands, wetlands

Wingspan: 1–1¼ in (2.6–3 cm)

Caterpillar length: ½ in (1.6 cm)

Butterfly lifespan: A few weeks

Diet: Leaves of rock-rose, bird's-foot trefoil, gorse, broom, bilberry, dogwood, bramble (caterpillar); flower nectar (butterfly)

The green hairstreak hibernates over winter as a pupa. It finds a safe home with the help of ants. The pupa makes squeaking sounds and produces sugary liquids to attract the ants. The ants either bury the pupa under soil or leaves, or carry it to their nest. This protects the pupa from the cold.

Like many butterflies, green hairstreaks sunbathe to warm up. Instead of opening out their wings to catch the Sun's rays, they keep them closed and tilt them at different angles, depending on the position of the Sun.

Madagascan sunset moth

Chrysiridia rhipheus

- The Madagascan sunset moth is named after the colors on its wings. From brilliant blue to deep orange, these seem like the sky as the Sun sets. The colors warn predators that the moth is poisonous, so they leave it alone.

- This insect looks more like a colorful butterfly than a moth. The sunset moth even flies during the day, like butterflies do. It also holds its wings up when it rests, rather than opening them out flat like a typical moth.

- The tails on the sunset moth's back wings look like the antennae on its head, so predators are not sure where the moth's real head is.

- Sunset moths migrate across the large island of Madagascar to find fresh plants for their caterpillars. Huge groups rest together at night for safety.

Fact file

Lives: Madagascar

Habitat: Deciduous forests, rainforests

Wingspan: 2¾–4¼ in (7–11 cm)

Lifespan: 8–12 weeks (caterpillar); moth not recorded

Diet: Spurge plants (caterpillar); flower nectar (moth)

The dark part of the sunset moth's wings has scales that contain black pigment. The bright, metallic colors are created by the way light is reflected through clear curved scales covering the rest of the wings.

Lobster moth caterpillar

Stauropus fagi

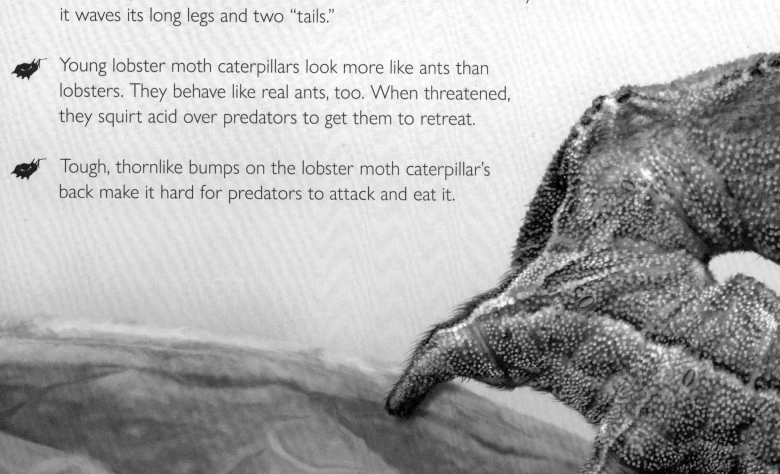

- Lobster moths are named after their caterpillars, which look like tiny lobsters when they try to scare predators away.

- To make itself look like a dangerous spider or scorpion to predators, the caterpillar arches its head and rear end back over its body. Then it waves its long legs and two "tails."

- Young lobster moth caterpillars look more like ants than lobsters. They behave like real ants, too. When threatened, they squirt acid over predators to get them to retreat.

- Tough, thornlike bumps on the lobster moth caterpillar's back make it hard for predators to attack and eat it.

In winter, the lobster moth caterpillar turns into a pupa and rests inside a strong silk cocoon. The cocoon is usually hidden among dead leaves on the woodland floor.

Female lobster moths lay their eggs on the leaves of many different kinds of trees in the summer months. When the caterpillars first hatch out, they feed on their own eggshells.

Fact file

Lives: Europe, Asia

Habitat: Deciduous woodlands

Wingspan: 1½–2¾ in (4–7 cm)

Caterpillar length: 2¾ in (7 cm)

Moth lifespan: Up to 6 weeks

Diet: Leaves of oak, beech, birch, hazel, chestnut and other trees (caterpillar); flower nectar (moth)

Cairns birdwing butterfly

Ornithoptera euphorion

🦋 The Cairns birdwing is Australia's largest native butterfly. It is also one of the largest in the world.

🦋 When they are feeding at flowers, these huge butterflies support their weight by beating their wings very quickly. Males sometimes drive small birds away from flowers so that they can keep all the nectar for themselves.

🦋 The female Cairns birdwing is much bigger than the male. Her black, white, and yellow colors are good camouflage in the dappled shade of her forest home.

🦋 The bright yellow and green colors of the male Cairns birdwing help him to attract a mate. He chases the female to show his colors off.

🦋 The female Cairns birdwing lays up to 300 eggs in her lifetime. She glues her eggs on or near pipevine leaves.

🦋 Cairns birdwing caterpillars feed on the leaves of two species of poisonous pipevines. They are not harmed by the poison and store it in orange spines, which deters predators from attacking them. The butterflies are poisonous, too.

🦋 The Cairns birdwing pupa is yellow and brown. It looks like a dried-up dead leaf—an effective camouflage that keeps it safe from predators.

Fact file

Lives: Queensland in Australia

Habitat: Rainforests, gardens

Wingspan: female: 6–7¾ in (15–20 cm); male: 5 in (13 cm)

Caterpillar length: 2½–3½ in (6.5–9 cm)

Butterfly lifespan: 4–5 weeks

Diet: Leaves of pipevines (caterpillar); flower nectar, rotting fruit (butterfly)

Painted lady butterfly

Vanessa cardui

 The painted lady is one of the most widespread butterflies in the world. It is also one of the few species of butterflies to have been recorded in Iceland.

 Painted lady butterflies are powerful fliers. They can reach speeds of 30 mph (50 kmph), which is as fast as a car usually travels in a town or a city.

 Instead of hibernating in winter, painted lady butterflies often migrate to find warmer weather, space, and food. They sometimes travel 100 miles (160 km) in one day. Large groups fly together, so the sky seems to be full of butterflies.

 Like other butterflies and moths, the painted lady sucks up nectar from flowers through a long, strawlike tube called a proboscis. This tube curls up underneath its head when it is not needed.

 Female painted ladies lay about 500 tiny green-gray eggs in just a few weeks. They visit lots of different kinds of plants, but lay just a single egg on each one.

Fact file

Lives: Africa, Asia, Europe, North, and Central America

Habitat: Meadows, fields, parks, marshes, scrublands, sand dunes, mountains

Wingspan: 2–2¾ in (5–7 cm)

Caterpillar length: 1¼– 2 in (3–5 cm)

Butterfly lifespan: 1–3 weeks

Diet: Leaves of thistle, nettle, sunflower, hollyhock, mallow (caterpillar); flower nectar (butterfly)

Painted ladies belong to a group known as "brush-footed" butterflies. This group is named after the brushlike tufts on the two small front legs of the males. Only the back four legs are used for walking.

Cinnabar moth

Tyria jacobaeae

The bright colors of cinnabar moths and their striped black-and-orange caterpillars are a warning to predators that they are poisonous and taste bitter.

Cinnabar moths are poisonous because their caterpillars eat a poisonous plant—ragwort. The caterpillars pass their poisons on to the adult moth.

The cinnabar moth is named after the mineral cinnabar, which is also red and poisonous. Cinnabar was once used by artists to make red paint.

Each of the cinnabar moth's large eyes has up to 6,000 separate lenses. The eyes are good at detecting movement.

Female cinnabar moths lay up to 300 eggs, usually in groups of 30–60. They lay them on the lower leaves of the ragwort plant.

Fact file

Lives: Europe, Asia, New Zealand, Australia, North America.

Habitat: Grasslands, sand dunes, heathlands, gardens, farmland, woodlands

Wingspan: 1¼–1¾ in (3.2–4.2 cm)

Caterpillar length: 1¼ in (3 cm)

Moth lifespan: 2–3 weeks

Diet: Ragwort leaves and flowers (caterpillar); flower nectar (moth)

Cinnabar moth caterpillars feed in large groups, feasting on ragwort leaves. They can quickly strip a whole plant completely bare.

When there is not enough food to go around, cinnabar moth caterpillars sometimes eat each other—they become cannibals.

Forest giant owl butterfly

Caligo eurilochus

The forest giant owl butterfly is named after the circles on its back wings, which look like an owl's eyes. Predators are scared off when they see the eyespots because they think they belong to an owl—a bigger and more dangerous animal.

Unusually for a butterfly, the forest giant owl is active at dawn and dusk. These huge butterflies cannot fly very far at any one time, so they are safer when the forest is darker, as it is harder for predators to spot them.

When the forest giant owl butterfly opens its wings, it shows patches of blue and purple. If the butterfly is threatened, it opens and shuts its wings quickly. The flashes of bright color startle predators, giving the butterfly time to escape.

Fact file

Lives: Central and South America

Habitat: Rainforests, banana plantations

Wingspan: 6¾–7¾ in (17–20 cm)

Caterpillar length: 6¼ in (16 cm)

Butterfly lifespan: 4 weeks

Diet: Heliconia, banana plants (caterpillar); flower nectar, rotting fruit, tree sap, animal dung (butterfly)

There are about 20 different species of owl butterflies. These spectacular creatures are endangered due to habitat loss and illegal trade, and so conservation measures need to be taken to ensure they do not become extinct.

These butterflies usually live on their own, but the caterpillars often gather in groups. They come out to feed at night.

Broad-bordered bee hawk-moth

Hemaris fuciformis

With its stripy, plump, hairy body, the broad-bordered bee hawk-moth looks more like a bumblebee than a moth. Because it seems like a creature that can sting, it is able to fly during the day in safety.

Bee hawk-moths are larger and more acrobatic in their flight than real bees. When they hover in front of flowers, their wings beat so fast that they look blurred and almost invisible.

Bee hawk-moth caterpillars have a purple stripe along their underside. This helps them to blend in with the purple stems of honeysuckle plants while they feed on the leaves. The caterpillars usually feed at night and rest during the day.

If the caterpillars are disturbed or feel threatened, they drop to the ground using a silk safety line. This is the quickest way for them to escape danger.

The bee hawk-moth pupa spends the winter hibernating in a silk cocoon buried just below ground.

When the bee hawk-moth emerges from its cocoon, its wings are covered in scales, like all butterflies and moths. After it flies for the first time, many of the scales drop off, leaving large, clear patches on the wings.

Fact file

Lives: North Africa, Europe, Asia

Habitat: Woodlands, heathlands, grasslands, gardens

Wingspan: 1½–2 in (3.8–4.8 cm)

Caterpillar length: 1½–1¾ in (4–4.5 cm)

Moth lifespan: 2–4 weeks

Diet: Leaves of honeysuckle, bedstraws, snowberry (caterpillar); flower nectar (moth)

Polyphemus moth caterpillar

Antheraea polyphemus

- When the Polyphemus moth caterpillar first hatches out of its egg, it is white with black stripes and has orange hairs on its back.

- Like all caterpillars, the Polyphemus moth caterpillar has to shed its skin, or molt, several times as it grows. It becomes bright green only when it is fully grown.

- This caterpillar is the juvenile, or developing, form of one of the largest silk moths in the world. It spins a tough layer of silk around its cocoon to protect itself as a pupa.

- Polyphemus moth caterpillars scare away predators by making a clicking sound with their mouthparts. They sometimes also vomit foul-tasting fluids and often rear up to make themselves look less like a caterpillar.

Fact file

Lives: North America, Mexico

Habitat: Deciduous woodlands, wetlands, parks, fields, gardens

Wingspan: 4–6 in (10–15 cm)

Caterpillar length: 2½–3 in (6–7.5 cm)

Lifespan: 1–2 months (caterpillar); less than a week (moth)

Diet: Leaves such as birch, oak, maple, willow, walnut, fruit trees (caterpillar); no food (moth)

These caterpillars have huge appetites, feeding on the leaves of over 50 different types of trees and shrubs.

Peacock butterfly

Aglais io

- The peacock butterfly is named after the eyespots on its wings, which are similar to the markings found on peacock feathers.

- When it closes its wings, the peacock butterfly hides its bright colors. The undersides of its wings look like a dead leaf, which helps the butterfly to camouflage itself in its surroundings.

- If it is disturbed, the peacock butterfly unfolds its wings to reveal four big eyespots. These make the butterfly look like a larger and fiercer animal.

- When they are threatened by predators such as mice or birds, peacock butterflies rub their wings together to make a hissing sound. This noise scares their attackers away.

- Peacock caterpillars are black and covered in spikes for protection. When they are about two weeks old, they gather together to spin a silk web. The caterpillars all live and feed inside this web for safety.

Fact file

Lives: Europe, Asia

Habitat: Woodlands, fields, meadows, gardens, parks, mountains

Wingspan: 2¼–2½ in (5.7–6.4 cm)

Caterpillar length: 1½ in (3.8 cm)

Butterfly lifespan: Up to 11 months

Diet: Nettle leaves (caterpillar); flower nectar, tree sap, rotten fruit (butterfly)

Peppered moth

Biston betularia

 The peppered moth is most commonly white with black speckles. It was given this name because it looks as if it has been sprinkled with black pepper.

 Peppered moths rest on tree trunks during the day with their wings spread open. Their speckled coloring gives them good camouflage against tree trunks covered in pale green lichens.

 There is a rarer type of peppered moth that is black with white speckles. These tend to be found in cities, where pollution makes the tree bark darker.

 Male peppered moths have thick, feathery antennae. These provide a large surface area to pick up the scent of female peppered moths.

Female peppered moths lay up to 2,000 tiny green eggs each summer.

Peppered moth caterpillars are masters of disguise. They look like twigs, with thornlike legs and a head like a broken stem. The caterpillars even slowly change their color, becoming green or brown to match their background.

Fact file

Lives: Europe, North America, Asia

Habitat: Woodlands, meadows, scrublands, hedgerows, parks, gardens

Wingspan: 1¾–2½ in (4.5–6.2 cm)

Caterpillar length: 2½ in (6 cm)

Moth lifespan: 8–12 months

Diet: Leaves of blackthorn, hawthorn, birch, oak, bramble, broom, rose (caterpillar); flower nectar, rotting fruit (moth)

Cleopatra butterfly

Gonepteryx cleopatra

- Cleopatra butterflies rest with their wings closed. The undersides look like green leaves with raised veins. This is useful camouflage from predators.

- Female Cleopatra butterflies are slightly bigger than the males and have pale yellow or greenish wings. The males are bright yellow, with orange patches on their front wings that show through to the undersides.

- The Cleopatra butterfly's colors come from waste products produced by its body. This is the same for all members of the *Pieridae* butterfly family, which are mostly white, yellow, or orange.

- Cleopatra butterflies hibernate during the winter. Their temperature drops and their life processes slow down, which helps them to survive the cold.

Fact file

Lives: North Africa, Mediterranean Europe, Middle East

Habitat: Open woodlands, scrublands, mountains, gardens

Wingspan: 2–2¾ in (5–7 cm)

Caterpillar length: ½–1½ in (1.5–4 cm)

Butterfly lifespan: Up to 10 months

Diet: Buckthorn leaves (caterpillar); flower nectar (butterfly)

Because it hibernates as an adult rather than a pupa, the Cleopatra butterfly is one of the first to appear in spring.
It is a strong flier, taking to the air as soon
as it is warm enough.

Red cracker butterfly

Hamadryas amphinome

- The red cracker butterfly is named after the underside of its wings, which are bright red. The top side of its wings are a brilliant blue color.

- Cracker butterflies are named after the crackling sound made by the wings of males when they take off. Scientists think the sound helps the males to defend their territory or attract females to mate with.

- To attract females, the male red cracker butterfly rests upside down on a tree trunk with his wings spread out flat. He makes clicking sounds to defend his territory from rival males.

- Red cracker butterflies do not feed on flower nectar like most other butterflies. They prefer to sip the juices from rotting fruit or to feast on animal dung.

Fact file

Lives: Central and South America, Southern USA

Habitat: Rainforests, dry forests

Wingspan: 3–3½ in (7.4–8.6 cm)

Caterpillar length: 1¼ in (3.2 cm)

Butterfly lifespan: About 2 weeks

Diet: Spurge leaves (caterpillar); rotting fruit, animal dung (butterfly)

The female red cracker hangs a chain of up to 15 eggs underneath a spurge leaf. The eggs hatch in about eight days.

The adult red cracker is quite a large butterfly. With its wings stretched out, it would just fit on the palm of an adult's hand.

Giant leopard moth

Hypercompe scribonia

 The giant leopard moth is named after the snow leopard. The moth's white color and hollow black spots look like the markings on a snow leopard's white fur coat.

 Giant leopard moths have ears where their back wings join onto the body. This helps the moths to detect the high-pitched hunting calls made by their main nighttime predator—bats.

 When threatened, giant leopard moths "play dead," because predators prefer to eat living animals. The moths often reveal their shiny blue-and-orange abdomen, or belly, to scare attackers away.

 Giant leopard moth males are almost twice the size of females.

Fact file

Lives: North, Central, and South America

Habitat: Woodlands, scrublands, gardens, parks

Wingspan: female: 2 in (5 cm); male: 3½ in (9 cm)

Caterpillar length: 3 in (7.5 cm)

Lifespan: Up to 3 years (caterpillar); a few days (moth)

Diet: Leaves of a variety of plants, including cabbage, sunflower, magnolia, banana, plantain, cherry, violet, dandelion (caterpillar); no food (moth)

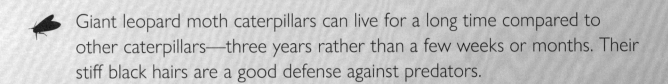 Giant leopard moth caterpillars can live for a long time compared to other caterpillars—three years rather than a few weeks or months. Their stiff black hairs are a good defense against predators.

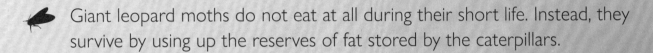 Giant leopard moths do not eat at all during their short life. Instead, they survive by using up the reserves of fat stored by the caterpillars.

Tawny coster butterfly

Acraea terpsicore

- Female tawny coster butterflies lay 20–100 eggs at a time. They usually glue the yellow eggs in tight clusters underneath plant leaves, but eggs can also be found on plant stems.

- If tawny coster butterflies are threatened by predators, they produce a poisonous yellow liquid from their leg joints and pretend to be dead. The poisons come from the plants that the caterpillars eat, such as passionflower vines.

- Tawny costers have managed to cross the Timor Sea from Indonesia to Australia—a distance of more than 400 miles (700 km). They are now spreading across Australia, with hundreds of them migrating together.

- As tawny costers get older, they shed some of the scales covering their leathery wings. This makes the wings look almost see-through in places.

Fact file

Lives: India, Sri Lanka, Southeast Asia, Australia

Habitat: Grasslands, scrublands, woodlands, parks, roadsides

Wingspan: 1½–2½ in (4–6.4 cm)

Caterpillar length: 1–1½ in (2.8–3.5 cm)

Lifespan: Up to 3 weeks (caterpillar); not recorded (butterfly)

Diet: Passionflower vines, spade flower, yellow alder, gourds (caterpillar); flower nectar (butterfly)

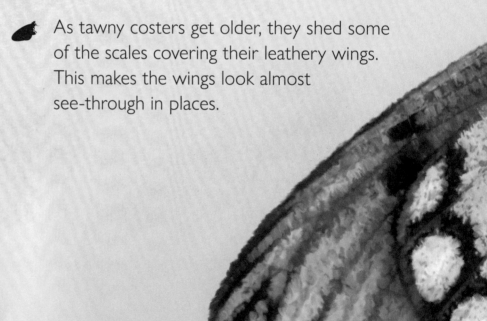

All butterflies have short, hairy stalks called palps on either side of their heads. They use these mouthparts to touch and taste things so that they can find food. The tawny coster's palps are bright yellow.

Orange oakleaf butterfly

Kallima inachus

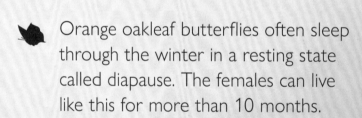

- The orange oakleaf butterfly's wings are vivid orange and purply blue on top and mottled brown underneath.

- The orange oakleaf butterfly looks like a dead leaf when its wings are closed. This is ideal camouflage for hiding among dead leaves on the forest floor. When feeding on tree sap, the butterfly hangs upside down, which makes it look even more like a dead leaf.

- The orange oakleaf emerges in both the dry season and the rainy season. The wings of dry season butterflies are light brown underneath. The rainy season butterflies have deeper-brown colors, which provide better camouflage among the darker wet leaves.

- Orange oakleaf butterflies often sleep through the winter in a resting state called diapause. The females can live like this for more than 10 months.

Fact file

Lives: East and South Asia

Habitat: Tropical forests, mountain forests

Wingspan: 3¼–4¼ in (8.5–11 cm)

Caterpillar length: ¾–1 in (1.7–2.7 cm)

Butterfly lifespan: 5–8 weeks

Diet: Leaves of nettle, knotweed, swampweed, Chinese foldwing, Persian shield (caterpillar); rotting fruit, tree sap, dung (butterfly)

The orange oakleaf is a strong flier. When it flies to escape birds, it is able to change direction suddenly. This confuses the birds, giving the butterfly time to escape and disappear among the fallen leaves.

Spanish moon moth

Graellsia isabellae

- The Spanish moon moth has four eyespots, each with a little moon-shaped white crescent. This is how it got its name.

- The Spanish moon moth caterpillar survives the cold mountain winters as a pupa inside a tough silk cocoon on the forest floor.

- Once it has hatched from its cocoon, the adult Spanish moon moth lives for only a few days. It uses this time to mate and lay eggs. It does not need to eat anything during its short life, so it has no mouthparts.

- Most butterflies and moths need warm weather to be able to fly, but the Spanish moon moth flies around even when nighttime temperatures are as low as 40°F (5°C).

Fact file

Lives: Spain, France, Switzerland

Habitat: Dry mountain pine forests

Wingspan: 2½–4 in (6–10 cm)

Caterpillar length: 2¾–3 in (7–8 cm)

Moth lifespan: About 1 week

Diet: Pine needles (caterpillar); no food (moth)

The tails at the end of the Spanish moon moth's back wings are twice as long in the males as they are in the females.

The Spanish moon moth is in serious danger of extinction. It is affected by climate change and the insecticides used to kill other insects in the places where it lives.

Garden tiger moth caterpillar

Arctia caja

- Garden tiger moth caterpillars are covered in long, fuzzy hairs. Caterpillars like these are known as "woolly bears."

- The caterpillar's hairs help to protect it from predators because they make it hard to swallow and digest. Some of the hairs give people skin rashes because they contain the chemical formic acid.

- The garden tiger moth caterpillar hibernates in winter and starts feeding again in spring. Its hairy body acts like a fur coat to keep out the winter cold.

Fact file

Lives: North America, Europe, Asia

Habitat: Grasslands, meadows, gardens, woodlands, sand dunes

Wingspan: 1½–3 in (4–7.6 cm)

Caterpillar length: 1½–2½ in (4–6 cm)

Lifespan: 8–9 months (caterpillar); 1–2 weeks (moth)

Diet: Leaves of nettle, thistle, willowherb, dock, plantain, and foxglove, fungi, dead animals (caterpillar); flower nectar (moth)

The garden tiger moth caterpillar feeds in groups to provide safety from predators. If it is disturbed, a caterpillar will curl up into a ball, which protects its soft underside.

Garden tiger moth caterpillars make thin, loose cocoons from their own hairs bound together with silk. Cocoons are hidden among dead leaves on the ground.

Garden tiger moths can detect the high-pitched squeaks of bats using ears on their thorax, or upper body. The moths also produce squeaking sounds, which warns bats to leave them alone because they are poisonous.

Postman butterfly

Heliconius melpomene

Postman butterflies live for up to six or even nine months. This is much longer than most other butterflies, which survive for only a few days or weeks. The reason for their long life is their diet. The postman feeds not just on nectar but also on pollen, which is very nutritious.

Postman caterpillars eat only one kind of plant—the passionflower. It is poisonous to other animals, but not to the caterpillars.

The black-and-orange coloring of postman butterflies warns predators that they are poisonous. The butterflies also give off a nasty smell when they sense danger.

At night, these butterflies rest together in large groups for protection. There are more of them to spot danger, and predators are confused about which butterfly to attack.

Fact file

Lives: Central and South America

Habitat: Forests

Wingspan: 2½–3¼ in (6.4–8.4 cm)

Caterpillar length: ½ in (1.3 cm)

Butterfly lifespan: 2–6 months, sometimes up to 9 months

Diet: Passionflower vines (caterpillar); pollen, flower nectar, ripe/rotting fruit (butterfly)

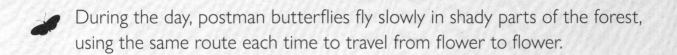 During the day, postman butterflies fly slowly in shady parts of the forest, using the same route each time to travel from flower to flower.

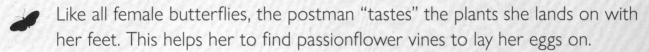 Like all female butterflies, the postman "tastes" the plants she lands on with her feet. This helps her to find passionflower vines to lay her eggs on.

Monarch butterfly

Danaus plexippus

◆ Monarch butterflies are famous for their long migrations. To escape the cold winters in North America, millions of them fly south together for up to 3,000 miles (5,000 km). They hibernate in Southern California or in the mountain forests of Mexico.

◆ Monarch butterflies only migrate in daylight. Scientists think they use the Sun or Earth's magnetic field to help them fly in the right direction.

◆ When the monarch first comes out of its chrysalis, its wings are crumpled and wet. It pumps fluids and air along the veins in its wings to stretch them out to their full size. Once the wings are dry, the butterfly can take flight.

◆ Monarch butterflies flap their wings slowly, at 5–12 times per second. Most butterflies flap their wings at about 20 times per second.

To attract females, male monarchs produce scents from the scales in the two black spots in the middle of their back wings.

 Monarch butterflies are now close to extinction. Conservationists are encouraging people to help boost their numbers by planting milkweed plants for the caterpillars and butterflies to feed on.

Fact file

Lives: North, Central, and northern South America, Caribbean, Australia, New Zealand, India, Philippines, Morocco, Europe

Habitat: Forests, mountains, fields, gardens, marshes, roadsides

Wingspan: 3–4 in (7.6–10.2 cm)

Caterpillar length: 2¾ in (7 cm)

Butterfly lifespan: 2–6 weeks; migrating butterflies, up to 9 months

Diet: Milkweed leaves (caterpillar); flower nectar, especially milkweed (butterfly)

Vampire moth

Calyptra minuticornis

- This moth gets its name because the male of the species drinks blood, like the vampires of myth and legend. There are many different kinds of vampire moth.

- This type of vampire moth feeds on the blood of mammals such as elephants, water buffalos, tapirs, rhinoceroses, deer, antelopes, and pigs. It sometimes feeds on human blood as well. This is uncomfortable but not harmful to people.

- The male vampire moth does not have sharp teeth like the vampires in horror films. Instead, he drills into the skin of mammals with his proboscis, or feeding tube, which is covered in sharp hooks and barbs.

- Scientists are not sure why the male vampire moth drinks blood. The salty blood could be a gift to the female during mating. The female then passes on the nutritious salt to the eggs she lays. This helps the caterpillars that hatch out of the eggs to thrive.

Fact file

Lives: South and Southeast Asia, Australia

Habitat: Forests, grasslands, scrublands

Wingspan: 1¾–2 in (4.5–5 cm)

Caterpillar length: 1½–2 in (3.5–5 cm)

Moth lifespan: 2–4 weeks

Diet: Moonseed leaves (caterpillar); fruit, flower nectar, mammal blood (moth)

This vampire moth is camouflaged to look like a dead leaf. Its disguise helps it to hide from predators such as birds and bats. This works best when the moth keeps perfectly still.

Both male and female vampire moths use their sharp proboscis to make holes in ripe fruit so they can drink the sugary juices.

Canadian tiger swallowtail butterfly

Papilio canadensis

- This butterfly gets its name because the long "tails" on its back wings look like the tails of birds called swallows.

- Like many other butterflies, Canadian tiger swallowtails gather around puddles in their hundreds to drink the muddy water. This water is rich in salts and other minerals.

- When they first hatch, Canadian tiger swallowtail caterpillars look like brown-and-white bird droppings. This clever disguise puts predators off eating them. As they grow, the caterpillars turn green and develop two false eyes, which help to scare predators away.

- If an older Canadian tiger swallowtail caterpillar detects a predator, it rears up and pops out two bright orange horns from its head. These horns look like a snake's forked tongue and give off a very unpleasant smell.

- The Canadian tiger swallowtail spends the winter resting as a pupa, without eating or drinking. Like other species from cold climates, it is protected from the low temperatures by a chemical "antifreeze" in its body.

- Male and female Canadian tiger swallowtails usually look the same, but a rare female form of this butterfly is all black.

Fact file

Lives: Canada, northern USA

Habitat: Deciduous woodlands, gardens

Wingspan: 2½–3 in (6.4–8 cm)

Caterpillar length: 2 in (5.5 cm)

Butterfly lifespan: 2–3 weeks

Diet: Leaves of birch, aspen, cherry, willow (caterpillar); flower nectar (butterfly)

Rosy maple moth

Dryocampa rubicunda

The rosy maple moth is the smallest member of the silk moth family. It is named after its striking bright pink color and the maple leaves its caterpillar feeds on. These moths are surprisingly well camouflaged among pink and red maple leaves, flowers, and seed cases.

Male rosy maple moths have long antennae that look like combs. These help the males to detect the special scent given off by females to attract a mate.

Rosy maple moths come out at night. This helps them to avoid predatory birds such as blue jays and black-capped chickadees, which hunt during the day.

Female rosy maple moths lay their yellow-green eggs in groups of 10–30 underneath maple leaves. The eggs hatch in about two weeks.

Although adult rosy maple moths are not poisonous, their bright colors trick predators into thinking they taste horrible and should be left alone.

Fact file

Lives: Eastern USA, southern Canada

Habitat: Deciduous woodlands, parks

Wingspan: 1¼-2 in (3.2–5.5 cm)

Caterpillar length: 2 in (5 cm)

Moth lifespan: About 1 week

Diet: Leaves of maple, oak (caterpillar); no food (moth)

The rosy maple moth caterpillar is nicknamed the "green-striped mapleworm." It is bright green with dark green stripes along its body.

65

American snout butterfly

Libytheana carinenta

 Snout butterflies are named after their long palps, or mouthparts. These stick out from the front of their head like a pointed snout.

 The American snout butterfly can cleverly hide itself from predators. It looks like a dead leaf when it rests with its wings folded. It also holds its snout and antennae together to look like a dead leaf stalk.

 When a predator is nearby, American snout butterflies sometimes startle them by flicking open their wings to reveal their bright orange color. This gives the butterfly time to escape.

 It takes just a couple of weeks for these butterflies to turn from an egg into an adult.

Fact file

Lives: North, Central, and South America

Habitat: Deciduous woodlands, gardens

Wingspan: 1¼–2 in (3.5–5 cm)

Caterpillar length: 1 in (2.5 cm)

Butterfly lifespan: About 2 weeks

Diet: Young hackberry leaves (caterpillar); rotting fruit, flower nectar (butterfly)

Sometimes, millions of these butterflies fly together looking for fresh food and mates. Scientists think this happens after heavy summer rains, which cause hackberry trees to grow lots of new leaves for the caterpillars to eat.

Eight-spotted forester moth

Alypia octomaculata

- This little moth is often mistaken for a butterfly because it flies during the day and sips nectar from flowers. However, its thick, hairy body is more like a moth's body than a butterfly's.

- The eight-spotted forester is named after the eight white patches on its wings. The moth reveals all eight spots when it opens its wings fully.

- The bright orange tufts on the eight-spotted forester's legs look a bit like the pollen baskets on a bee's legs. Scientists are not sure what these tufts are for.

- Eight-spotted foresters have a fast, darting flight. This helps them to avoid predators that hunt by sight, such as birds.

Fact file

Lives: Eastern USA, Canada, Mexico

Habitat: Woodlands, fields

Wingspan: 1–1½ in (2.5–3.8 cm)

Caterpillar length: ¾–1½ in (2.2–3.8 cm)

Moth lifespan: 2–10 weeks

Diet: Leaves of grapevines, Virginia creeper (caterpillar); flower nectar (moth)

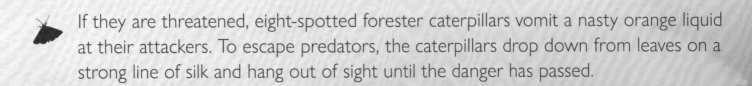 If they are threatened, eight-spotted forester caterpillars vomit a nasty orange liquid at their attackers. To escape predators, the caterpillars drop down from leaves on a strong line of silk and hang out of sight until the danger has passed.

This moth spends the winter as a pupa, hiding in the soil or in the cracks of soft, rotting wood. It can remain a pupa for several years.

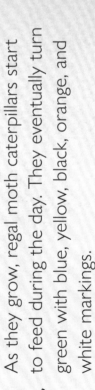

Regal moth caterpillar

Citheronia regalis

The regal moth caterpillar's nickname is the "hickory horned devil." This is because of the hickory tree leaves this enormous caterpillar likes to eat and the long, spiky horns on its head.

Although regal moth caterpillars look alarming to predators, they are harmless. Their horns and spines are not poisonous or sharp, but flies, wasps, and bats are likely to leave them alone.

When the caterpillars first hatch out, they are mostly black and look like bird droppings. At this stage, they feed at night and curl up on top of leaves during the day.

As they grow, regal moth caterpillars start to feed during the day. They eventually turn green with blue, yellow, black, orange, and white markings.

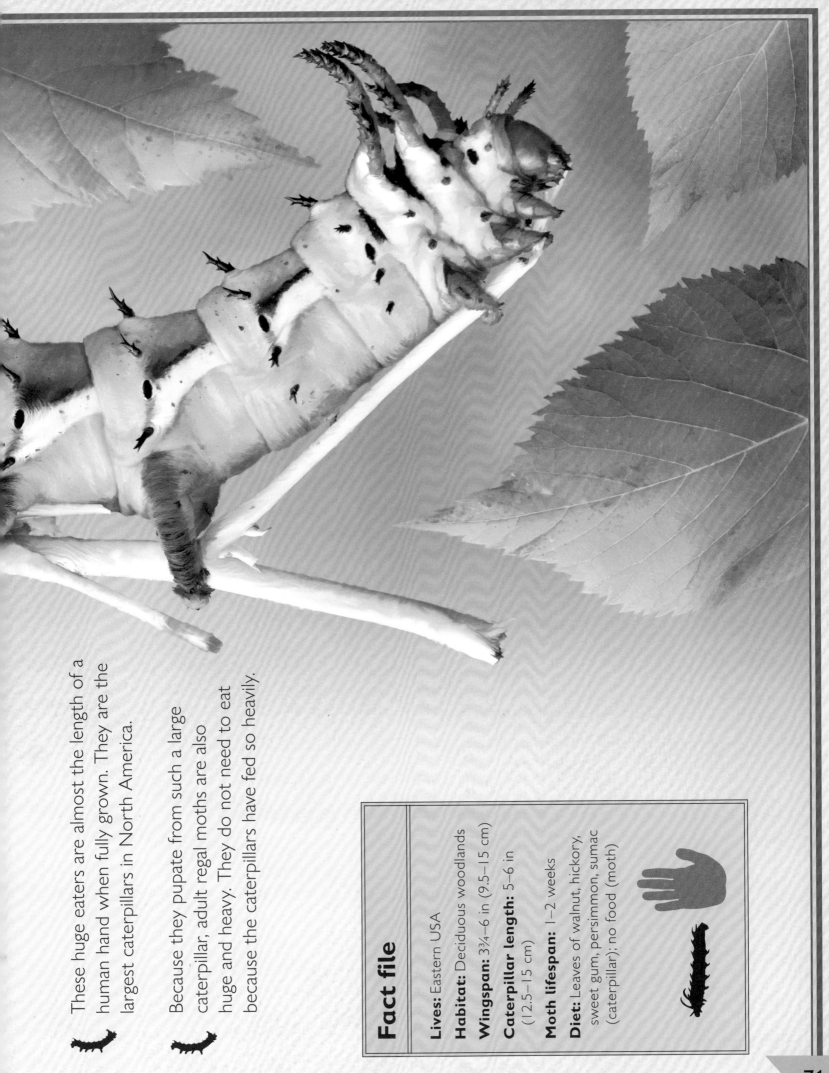

These huge eaters are almost the length of a human hand when fully grown. They are the largest caterpillars in North America.

Because they pupate from such a large caterpillar, adult regal moths are also huge and heavy. They do not need to eat because the caterpillars have fed so heavily.

Fact file

Lives: Eastern USA

Habitat: Deciduous woodlands

Wingspan: 3¾–6 in (9.5–15 cm)

Caterpillar length: 5–6 in (12.5–15 cm)

Moth lifespan: 1–2 weeks

Diet: Leaves of walnut, hickory, sweet gum, persimmon, sumac (caterpillar); no food (moth)

Salt marsh moth

Estigmene *acrea*

The salt marsh moth is a member of the tiger moth family—it is related to the garden tiger moth. They both have a very hairy caterpillar.

Salt marsh moths are mostly white with black spots. Their abdomens, or bellies, are yellow. Females have white back wings, whereas the back wings of the males are yellowy orange.

When threatened, salt marsh moths often drop to the ground, bring their wings up, and produce bad-smelling chemicals. These chemicals come from the plants that the caterpillars eat.

Fact file

Lives: North America, Mexico, Colombia, Kenya, Democratic Republic of the Congo

Habitat: Woodlands, fields, meadows, marshes, grasslands

Wingspan: 1¾–2¾ in (4.5–6.8 cm)

Caterpillar length: 2 in (5 cm)

Moth lifespan: Up to 4–5 days

Diet: Leaves of apple, walnut, cabbage, dandelion, potato, maize, clover (caterpillar); no food (moth)

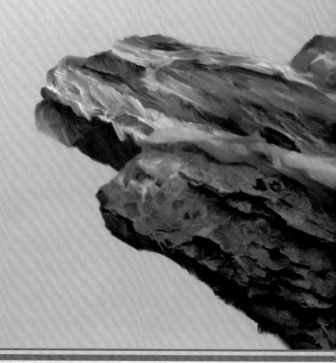

Male salt marsh moths have two hairy, curved tubes called coremata hidden inside their abdomens. These give off a scent to attract females for mating.

Older salt marsh moth caterpillars are unusally fast movers. They travel together in large groups to look for more food or a safe place to make a cocoon.

Female salt marsh moths lay their eggs in one or two clusters. A cluster can contain as many as 1,200 eggs.

Long-tailed skipper butterfly

Urbanus proteus

- Long-tailed skippers are named after the long "tails" on their back wings. Predators often take a bite out of these tails, but skippers can survive even if one or both of their tails are missing.

- Skipper butterflies get their name because of the way they fly. They dart quickly and jerkily from flower to flower and look as if they are skipping. This is different from the slow, graceful, gliding flight of most butterflies.

- The tips of the long-tailed skipper's antennae are hooked. A typical butterfly's antennae end in thickened clubs.

- Female long-tailed skippers lay their pale yellow eggs under leaves one at a time or in small stacks, one on top of the other.

- Long-tailed skipper caterpillars are sometimes called "bean leafrollers." They get this name from the way they roll up leaves so that they can feed inside them safely.

- The long-tailed skipper pupa has a powdery white surface, which scientists think makes it taste nasty to predators.

Fact file

Lives: Central and South America, Southern and Eastern USA

Habitat: Fields, meadows, woodlands, gardens, roadsides, coastal dunes

Wingspan: 1¾–2½ in (4.5–6 cm)

Caterpillar length: 1 in (2.5 cm)

Butterfly lifespan: 2–3 weeks

Diet: Leaves of beans, hog peanuts, butterfly peas, wisteria (caterpillar); flower nectar (butterfly)

Baltimore checkerspot butterfly

Euphydryas phaeton

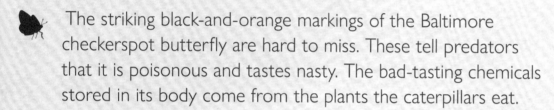 The striking black-and-orange markings of the Baltimore checkerspot butterfly are hard to miss. These tell predators that it is poisonous and tastes nasty. The bad-tasting chemicals stored in its body come from the plants the caterpillars eat.

 While they are feeding on nectar, Baltimore checkerspot butterflies spread their wings to show off their bright warning colors. This helps to stop predators, such as birds, from eating them.

Female Baltimore checkerspots lay clusters of 100–700 eggs under the leaves of white turtlehead plants.

Fact file

Lives: North America

Habitat: Wet meadows, bogs, marshes, grasslands, wooded hillsides, dry fields

Wingspan: 1¾–2¾ in (4.5–7 cm)

Caterpillar length: 1 in (2.5 cm)

Lifespan: 10–11 months (caterpillar); 3–4 weeks (butterfly)

Diet: Leaves of white turtlehead, plantain, honeysuckle, arrowwood (caterpillar); flower nectar, dung, dead animals (butterfly)

Unlike most butterflies and moths, the Baltimore checkerspot survives the cold winter months by resting as a caterpillar instead of a pupa. It hides on the ground among dead leaves, which it rolls together with silk.

The survival of the Baltimore checkerspot is threatened. Scientists are working hard to protect its habitat. They are also breeding these butterflies in captivity and releasing them into the wild to increase their numbers.

Rattlebox moth

Utetheisa ornatrix

- This small moth is named after the poisonous rattlebox plants that the caterpillars eat. Other names for this moth include the ornate moth, the bella moth, and the ornate bella moth.

- Both the adult rattlebox moth and its caterpillar have bright salmon-pink colors that tell predators they are poisonous. The eggs and the pupa are also poisonous.

- Most moths fly at night, but the rattlebox moth flies during the day. It can do so relatively safely because it is protected from daytime predators by its warning colors.

- Rattlebox moth caterpillars first feed on rattlebox leaves, then tunnel into unripe rattlebox pods to feed on the seeds inside. The seeds contain five times more poison than the leaves.

- The female mates with several males during her life—sometimes as many as 13.

- Each time they mate, the males give the females a "gift" of nutrients and poisons to pass on to their eggs. The extra nutrition allows the females to lay more eggs.

Fact file

Lives: North, Central, and South America

Habitat: Fields, forest edges, coasts

Wingspan: 1¼–1¾ in (3–4.5 cm)

Caterpillar length: 1¼–1½ in (3–3.5 cm)

Moth lifespan: 3–4 weeks

Diet: Leaves and seed pods of rattlebox plants (caterpillar); no food (moth)

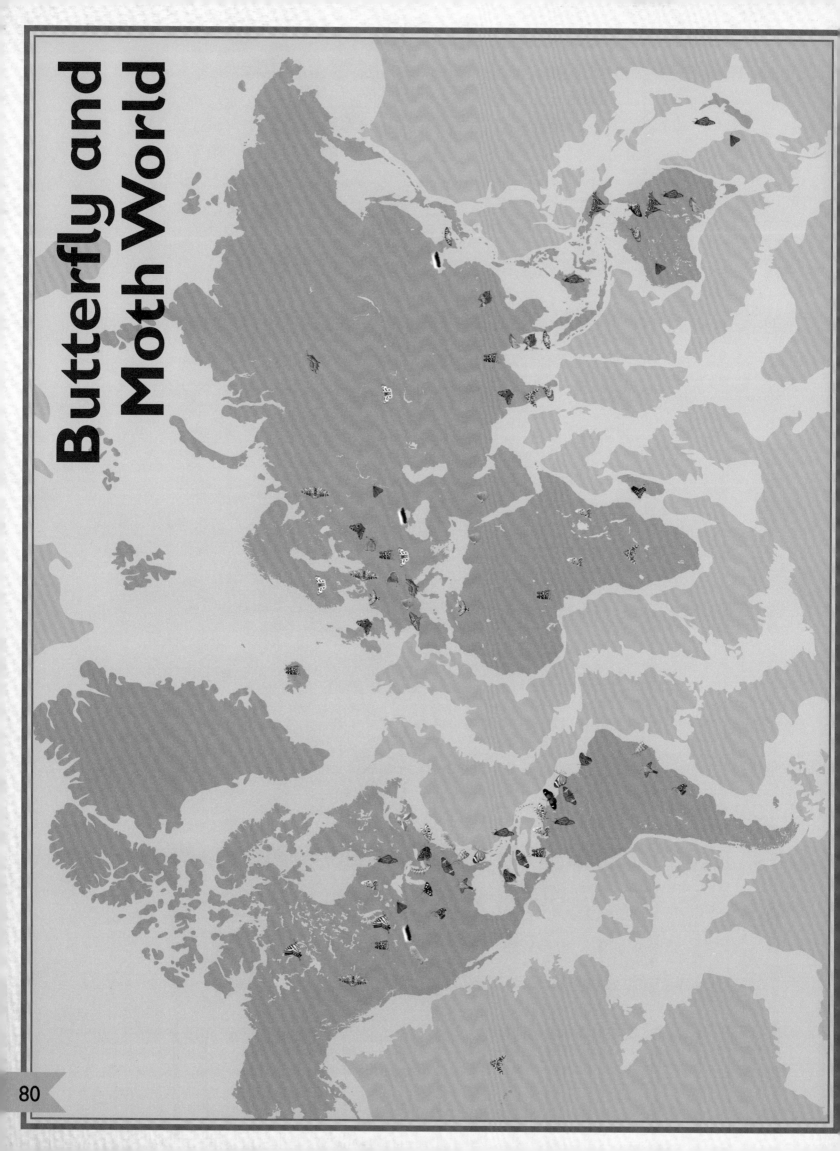